The Ghost Hospital
Pauline Rowe

Maytree Press 2019

Published 2019 by Maytree Press

www.maytreepress.co.uk

Copyright © Pauline Rowe 2019

ISBN: 978-1-9160381-7-2

A CIP catalogue record of this book is available from the
British Library.

Cover image: Abandoned © Kevin Threlfall

Maytree 008

Printed in the UK by PiggyPrint

Acknowledgements

Thanks to the editors of the following publications in which some of these poems first appeared: *The Fat Damsell Poems to Survive In, Coast to Coast to Coast, Morphrog, Ink, Sweat and Tears, Tilt 1:3 (Open Eye Gallery, Liverpool, 2018), Sleeping in the Middle (Open Eye Gallery, Liverpool, 2018), Stripe (Templar Poetry, 2009)* and *Skein (Templar Poetry, 2014).*

Many of these poems were written as part of PhD research at the University of Liverpool. Thanks to Yoko Ono for providing the John Lennon Memorial scholarship that enabled me to study, and to my supervisors Professor Deryn Rees-Jones and Professor David Pilgrim for their support. Thanks also to my examiners Professor John McAuliffe and Professor Jill Rudd.

I am also grateful to staff at Open Eye Gallery, Liverpool especially Sarah Fisher who gave me the chance to be the first writer-in-residence at the gallery. Thanks also to AJ Wilkinson for our exhibition, *Sleeping in the Middle.*

The gift of time, to write, is only possible because of the steadfast support of my husband, John and the tolerance of my children. Thank you.

For John and our children,
who know who they are x

Contents

The Ghost Hospital

It looks hospital.

Regulation beds. Stamped sheets.
People who know the code. Different tunics.
Pink, grey, green, teal.
Black and blue.

*

Greyscale light. Everything crashes
back: a waxy woman
walks the corridor   pauses

stops
        stands from breakfast
to lunch

at night when lights go out
but never quite completely

her batteries spark
she halts in surprise at her
own animated shout

"I'm a bit of a miracle!"
an index of memory.

At the shift change the building rises
from shallow footings,
            floats

on space between its floors and earth –

I see a crowd of women trapped
who can't return a look –

who dissolve particle by particle
as breath turns to whispered words,
words to water and tissue to dust,
solute, solvent, solution.

Our own mad
people invisible in plain sight.

A Madhouse Air

Mr. Dickens couldn't stand
the terrible crowd – in 1842;

words, exasperations, circumlocutions,
parentheses fixed from his inky pain,
across the Atlantic, home to London,
Paris to Gad's Hill and back again.

At La Saltpetrière,
the maniac points his finger
at the guards in vain.

In Kreuzlingen private sanatorium
the better class pick and touch torn
faces. Mouths are little 'O's of hell, men
with bony hands pull lips like chicken skin.

…terribly painful,
everything had a madhouse air.

Brentwood, New York
where Allen Ginsberg's mother died.

At Overbrook, 24 patients froze to death in bed,
gaslight shadows, arms of silver trails,
holes – a thumb's width –
left in hollow faces.

Topeka State Hospital, Kansas
54 men castrated like cattle,
walked in circles searching for their names:

catalogues of stolen souls in bricks –
their minds extracted – stored in slated roofs,
brown teeth and bitten nails
between the walls and greasy tiles.

McLean's, Massachusetts
with its famous roll call –

David Foster Wallace, Ray Charles,
Robert, Anne, Sylvia,
John Nash, James Taylor

...*this sad refuge of degraded humanity* –

each in their lonely days when
they could not find a friend.

Tell-tale

A doctor slices tissue from my tongue
releases rising rifts of shaken sound
defies the broken skin to leave me bound
up, silent, touched; he keeps the cords of song:

dumbstruck ventriloquized ageusiac
I pray my body's grace will seal the wound
for benedictions from St Blaise, confound
the fix from Astra Zeneca and Roche.

Raw wool against my spit
                stopped every noun.
A week of artful deaths, reprieve and sorrow
Have you come to kill us? – words I borrow

though not yet cleansed of love, nor speech nor sound
unsure which portion cast me from the fold –
the biter, top, the tip, its pull or hold.

Inclusive Arts

Today, we have drama for the marginalized,
training for community life –

please make yourselves comfortable.

The film in the glass is rain, March rain,
no dappled thing, no rose-moles sour or sweet.

The man who crouches in the corner commands
me, charter a peace bus across the freshly varnished floor.

The photographer in the kitchen hatch claims to be a king.
There's a dancer in the window, a cyclist at the door.

A tyrant in the cupboard with questions
I dare not answer.

What is inheritance?
Where is the border?

The Ward at Night

The women all want cigarettes.
Each of us has left the world,
electric light is low but never out.

The madhouse stripped of colour,
occupants drugged dull and duller
the mask of night is on my face.

The phone is full no breathing space
like messages, regrets
small change locked tight.

We line the corridors in disgrace
The grave's a fine and private place.
Like stations of the cross we wait, kowtow.

Blue's a name for health and many songs.
All the people we used to know
illusions to us now.

Long gone exemplars of remembrance –
real, unreal, vision, dream – hidden in our shames;

for one, I made an imprint of her face
gathered in cloth, pressed after love;
rain falling on my shoe. A snowy dove.

Then, an attic prophet, I named my birds:
Baby, Periwinkle, Navy Knickers, Electric,
Pufnstuf, Cornflower, Catweazle, Cobalt,

Crystal Gayle, Sky Blue, Joni and Miles, Sleep-tight,
Mother's Pride, Omo, Dolly Blue, Midnight.

Treatment

I seem a little manic
for a home-grown grimalkin.

I stalk shadows through the night.
Day by day my limbs grow thinner.

I've an instinct that an anaesthetic deep
inside me might be triggered

by the pressure of my head.

He hurls a stick for me to catch.

I bring the cold mouse
killed the night before.

He takes it by the tail, commanding *Fetch*.
I feel a little blood rise in each paw.

I force my skull
against the doctor's leg.

I scratch the wooden arm
of his consulting chair.

I love each sharpened claw.

He puts a collar round my neck,
my throat catches on a tiny fist of fur.

I'm a breathing curlicue. I lie down
inside a yellow pool of setting sun.

(I see the master has fine whiskers
yet he cannot see the cat in me.)

I smell the scuttling muck – approaching dark.
I cry – call out – I try to bark.

No one in the world can hear me now.
Meow. Meow. Meow. Meow.   Meow.

Personality Disorder

I need to say this
though you're six years dead,
though your lover's retired
from the operating theatre.

She won her knowledge
in the manner of privilege
like stolen carrion
from a 3 week training stint
on a psych ward –
preferred stitch-up medicine.

About me and my scars,
you were both wrong.

My personality is as ordered
as a breviary

it sings *Lord of the Dance*
every time it remembers death

recites the Quadratic formula
each blue morning –

it's as ordered as a heart
that's been broken
by Antarctic parents
then glued together
with the drool of donkeys
by Betsy Trotwood.

My obese personality
is an anarchist on Fridays.

It collects rejections,
transforms
them when asleep
into Cornell shadow boxes,
and divining rods
made from twigs
and acorn caps.

It refuses to smoke
adulterated tea or wear a cow-bell.

It tolerates insults, limericks
and text messages from institutions.

People say my personality
has nice hair because
it makes rug mats
out of vows, confesses more
perfectly than a scalpel –

it knows what it doesn't know,
and keeps its mouth shut
like a locked door
on an acute ward.

Cutting the Stone

(after Hieronymus Bosch)

He longs for sleep, it drives him
to wander the open fields — escape
the threat of gryllos in ecclesiastical gloom.

The destitute man reaches the tribunal
beneath the open summer sky
where those with power hold instruments
of small theatre; a red book and a pouring jug.

A surgeon and a monk attend, assisted by a nun
who wears the book upon her head.

They bind each subject to a chair,

monk and nun pretend to pray
a mime of incantations,

the surgeon drills the skull,
in which a tulip bulb pretends
to be a stone

through which the victim's heart
is terrified,

in which the stone pretends
to hold the key

to start the spark of folly.

Self-portrait

I was cut out
of a picture book
in 1963

made to stand
at the top of the class
clean, unloveable.

My minds were cut
out too; mother snipping
along dotted lines

to offer a choice of fittings.

Never able to choose
I just left both minds
bumping against each

other like tethered boats.

The Confusions of Father Christmas

The spring morning smugness in his ears
full of humming pigeons on the roof.

His mouth is dry and though the copper kettle
is still warm to touch, it holds no water.

Tears of dirt negotiate his beard,
he searches with his fingertips

for the small cruel lice he feels
dancing on his face.

The green velvet jacket does not fit
over his frayed and friable shirt.

A creature lows at his door
but does not know the designation – guide.

Without any care, how might he gather
these many sacks of sanctifications,

sufferings in every room
all over the house, if this is his house?

He sets a most reluctant course, closes his front door,
leaves an arc of unpaid bills around the mat.

Making Faces

watching 'R.D.Laing Has No Face' on YouTube

You look like a fine,
Russian dancer
or mime artist.

Do you follow the news
in the dark or shadow land –
can you hear us think about you?

When we read your books
are you released
from some small agony?
Like a plenary indulgence?

I watch your face become
your mother's face
- what you remembered
as your mother's face

how you try to emulate
her mask of sorrow,
in your own features

the expression that flooded
her cruel face, one rare day –
when your father brought home
a birthday gift, a small box
within a larger box;

anticipation deliberately engineered
for his pleasure,

fragments of him,
ten cut toe-nails
from his hard, dirty feet.

Pilgrim

after Tom Wood
for my son, leaving Liverpool, Jan 2018

"the Photo mat always turns you into a criminal type wanted by the police"
Roland Barthes

The first time I took you
further than the local shops
my skin was still loose
my bones precarious,

on our first morning journey to the river
through the exhalations and dirt
of the bus terminus

to a café where old men
face the same way without speaking

I took you to sit in a machine,
turned a potty-plastic seat
to its highest setting

closed a rough textured curtain
to record my disappearing face.

Look how separate we were, even then.

You – balanced on my lap
wrapped up tight against the cold.

I took time to read instructions
thinking how good it was
that no one could see
my uncertainty or fear.

You were my infant accomplice, my alibi.

I held you close and waited –
four identical frames appeared,
upside down, damp.

Like all new mothers
I needed to find an image
to study and imitate,

to avoid detection.

Patrimony

When she died they buried me with her,

they buried her as dead as I was quick,

when her body's flesh began to melt – mandible, ribs, femur, clavicle –

I heard curses, like serpents on a petrifying head
(an ounce, a hiss of tempest fuelled the cell).

The rot breathed in breathed out along and through

the punishment of bones.

I felt forcefulness of atmosphere, tested the timber's dark

resistance

dampened with exhalations – slow, swollen gasps of air.

I sang along the humerus, scattered fun-sized leaves

in metastatic ecstasies.

I weakened the constraint

     a steady shove of hatred pushed the lid

     welcomed in shadow-light of a day's dawn,

     dissolved the barricade.

     I rejoiced,

          excavated outwards   upwards, felt

    the warm earth against my corium

how I started again, stealthily

     (little buttermilk mouldy warp)

how I landed in the fresh, bright day in contemplation of another home.

Bequest

I bequeath him my skull
(inside which he leads another life),

my hip bones, the roots of my teeth, my scars,
the ones tight with secrets like lieder,
the ones that ache when it rains.

I go back in dreams to that cold kitchen,
stirring porridge on a 2-ring stove.

I didn't see the devil that winter
nor dress even the smallest tree.

I forgot the accommodations of ribbons
though there was frost enough for two.

It replays itself, his head to one side,
playful, keeping his word, so real
I can taste his breath.

My desire then was a pearl –
perfect, no start, no end, no memory of grit.

Late Meeting

When you asked about
ballistic stretching with Thera-Bands
I knew there was no future in it.

I asked you to repeat the words
just for the pleasure of your voice.
I paid my way and left the tip.

All the way home I assured myself
that twenty years changes a face:

without the fright-wig and pan-stick
I couldn't be sure it was you.

All the peace I've known

I am not able to give you co-ordinates
for that still hushed, drenched-with-hope place.
I stood there once,
yes - it was in Gloucestershire.
I remember.

I could hear birdsong -
but not all the birds of the county.

On a small bridge above the Wye
not far from Symond's Yat,
evening rain pitted the river,
a confetti of light touched my face,
like ashes at the start of Lent.

In the rented farmhouse
my lost friends prepared supper,
potato soup and solace with brown bread.

In my body, my bones prepared themselves
like a tailor's pattern
for the sons and daughters I could not imagine.

I did not know about the lilac light
(when all the world's asleep)
except for my baby and the mother I would be:
how I cradled my daughter
the way we should all be held.

I fed her with myself.

How like us to become food
and not know our powers.

How like peace to sit inside us.
To wait for that moment
of astonishment
when we open our mouths and sing.

Residents

But all the bloomy
flush of life
is here.

I rejoice
to find a pillow
for my shattered head.

In this place it is
the blessed pledge
of everyone
more bent to raise
the wretched
than to rise.

From spendthrift
to broken soldier,
we ask our guests
to sing for us –

willow girl
and wounded,
sing for us,

grieving widow,
forgetter,
father-frail sing for us,

voice and spirit follower,
witch and wanderer,
sing for us,

fast talker, fool,
flake and freak,
sing for us,

ever-hungry,
Feste, clown,
half-wit, ass
sing for us,

worry-worrier,
constant washer,
non-talker, howling man,
compulsive scribbler,
sing for us.

Head case,
cuckoo, dullard,
nut and radge,
commune with us.

Zany, banana,
maniac,
nincompoop,
commune with us.

Moon-struck,
simpleton,
fruit and kook,
poltroon and loon,
commune with us.

Screw-ball, cake,
let old things break
commune with us.

You too can claim
a kindred here and
have your claims allowed.

(If I could remember
how I got here
I would send a map
though you will know
this place by the fireside
you can sit beside,
open door and touch
that's neither
paid for nor begrudged,
the extra chair
at the table,
water freely shared,
where walls
are without mirrors
and no-one wears a watch.)

Here it is
the blessed pledge
of everyone
more bent to raise
the wretched
than to rise.

Notes

'A Madhouse Air' – Mr. Dickens is Charles Dickens and an account of his visit to Blackwell Island can be found in his American Notes, first published in 1842.

'Tell-tale' – St Blaise is known for the blessing of throats. 'Have you come to kill us?" is a reference to Christ curing the madman (Luke 4: 31 - 37).

'The Ward at Night' includes a line from Shakespeare's Romeo and Juliet and a line from Andrew Marvel's 'To his Coy Mistress.'

'Pufnstuf' is a reference to the 1970s children's TV programme 'H R Pufnstuf'.

The italicised lines in 'Residents' are taken from Oliver Goldsmith's poem 'The Deserted Village.'

About the Author

Pauline Rowe, was born and raised in Widnes. She has lived and worked in Liverpool for most of her adult life. She has been published in anthologies and magazines, including The Rialto, Smoke, The Reader, The Frogmore Papers, Staxtes etc., Her pamphlet *Playing Out Time* was published by Drift-wood Publications, her first collection *Waiting for the Brown Trout God* was published by Headland Publications. In 2014 Lapwing Publications published her collection, *Voices of the Benares.* Her collaborative exhibition *Sleeping in the Middle* – recorded poems in response to photographs by AJ Wilkinson – was shown at Open Eye Gallery, Liverpool, May 2018. Her latest ongoing collaborative work *The Allotments* – with photographic artist David Lockwood and artist, the late Arthur Lockwood – was shown as part of the LOOK Biennial exhibition at the Victoria Gallery and Museum in Liverpool, September 2019. Pauline has worked as Poet-in-Residence with Mersey Care NHS Foundation Trust since 2013 and was the first Writer-in-Residence with Open Eye Gallery, Liverpool (2016 – 2018). She is an associate tutor in creative writing at Edge Hill University